GO GREEN!

Written by
Liz Gogerly

Illustrated by
Miguel Sanchez

free spirit
PUBLISHING®

Published in North America by Free Spirit Publishing Inc., Minneapolis, Minnesota, 2019

Library of Congress Cataloging-in-Publication Data
This book has been filed with the Library of Congress.
ISBN-13: 978-1-63198-430-3

Free Spirit Publishing does not have control over or assume responsibility for author or third-party websites and their content.

Reading Level Grade 4; Interest Level Ages 8–12;
Fountas & Pinnell Guided Reading Level S

10 9 8 7 6 5 4 3 2 1
Printed in China
H13770319

Free Spirit Publishing Inc.
6325 Sandburg Road, Suite 100
Minneapolis, MN 55427-3674
(612) 338-2068
help4kids@freespirit.com
www.freespirit.com

First published in 2018 by Franklin Watts, a division of Hachette Children's Books · London, UK, and Sydney, Australia

Copyright © The Watts Publishing Group, 2018

The rights of Liz Gogerly to be identified as the author and Miguel Sanchez as the illustrator of this Work have been asserted in accordance with the Copyright, Designs and Patents Act, 1988.

Managing editor: Victoria Brooker

Design: Anthony Hannant (Little Red Ant)

Contents

The Birthday Party

The children have had a great time at Anjali's birthday party. They played party games like scavenger hunts and musical chairs, and there were lots of great prizes. Afterward they had a water balloon fight.

The party food was delicious, with plenty of treats for everyone. And Anjali loved unwrapping all her presents. All in all, it was a lot of fun but now there's a HUGE mess! And that has made the children stop and think . . .

What a mess!

Great present, but so much trash!

▲ Fred the Ted

This teddy bear is a great gift today, but what will happen to him in the future? Follow his journey through the book.

Plastic toys ▲

Plastic toys cannot be recycled and usually end up in landfills or polluting our oceans. Cheap plastic party favors are usually not made from the kind of plastic that will ever biodegrade.

▲ Balloons

Balloons can be great fun at a party, but it's important to never let them go outside. They eventually return to land or into the sea. Many animals, birds, and fish mistake them for food and this can kill them. Most balloons are not easily biodegradable and last for years.

We left a lot of food.

What happens to all the garbage?

Food waste ▲

Did you know that about one third of food that is produced in the world for humans to eat is wasted? All that food we throw away could be used to feed other people. Also, if we didn't waste so much, we could cut back on the resources we need to produce our food—such as energy, water, and land.

5

What Happens to Our Trash?

Anjali's party was just the beginning for these children. Next, they wanted to know what happened to those sacks filled with food and paper plates. Noah told them about a book from school that said our trash and garbage are taken to landfill sites. These are big holes in the ground where our waste is dumped.

Many households mix household waste with recyclable materials. All of this counts as household waste and it will go to landfills or be incinerated.

Trash bags
Some plastic trash bags can take up to 1,000 years to degrade. We can buy degradable trash bags that break down fully and harmlessly.

TAKE ACTION!

Go green in your own home! Sort all your waste before it goes into the trash. If your family members do not recycle, introduce the idea to them.

Incinerator ▲

The alternative to putting trash in landfill sites is to burn or incinerate our waste. Energy or electricity can be generated from the heat that is created.

STOP AND THINK!

Once a landfill site is full, it is covered with a clay or plastic liner followed by a layer of soil. Grass is often planted on top to make it look good. However, underground all kinds of things are happening. As food waste decomposes, it creates methane gas. This can be extracted and burned to create energy. Other gases and toxins that are made can be harmful as they leak into the surrounding air, water, and soil.

Landfills

♻ Some food will degrade in weeks, but plastic and glass may be in landfill sites for thousands of years.

♻ Aluminum cans take 80 to 200 years to break down in landfills, but these could be recycled.

♻ Disposable diapers can take 250 to 500 years to decompose.

♻ Paper will take just 2 to 6 weeks to decompose, but it could easily be recycled.

♻ An orange will decompose within 6 months.

♻ A banana peel will be gone in a month.

7

Go Green in the Countryside

The children begin thinking of more examples of how people do not dispose of their waste properly. Noah remembers when he went to a music festival in the countryside. His family arrived early and pitched their tent in a field. Everything was so green and beautiful. More people arrived with all their camping gear and boxes of food and drink. The festival lasted two days. Everyone had a good time, but afterward the field was a HUGE mess.

The four Rs

A festival can be clean, green fun if we remember to **r**educe, **r**euse, **r**ecycle, and take **r**esponsibility.

Wow, I love the outdoors.

MUSIC FESTIVAL

TAKE ACTION!

Protecting the natural environment and not harming animals, birds, plants, or trees is important. Most countries have a list of rules you should follow when you visit the countryside or wilderness areas. Number one is to leave no trace of your visit and take all your litter home.

STOP AND THINK!

Estimated time for everyday items to decompose:

- glass bottles: 1 to 2 million years
- leather shoes: 25 to 40 years
- rubber rain boots: 50 to 80 years
- nylon or synthetic fibers used in tents: 30 to 40 years

After the festival . . .

What have we done?

The fifth R is respect

Everyone can enjoy the outdoors if we all remember to respect the living things around us. But if we trample on plants and flowers, some animals and insects will lose their natural habitats.

9

Love Our Planet

Have you ever had a "wake-up moment" about the environment like these children did? Did you suddenly realize that the everyday things you do have an impact on the world? Anjali, Noah, Lulu, and Mason decide they want to take more responsibility and look after our planet. But why is it important to take action *now*?

Our oceans

Things we throw away may contribute to the Great Pacific Garbage Patch floating in the ocean. This drifting pile of trash is believed to be the size of India, Mexico, and Europe combined. Much of this trash is plastic that will not decompose. Plastic waste, including plastic bags, kills around 1 million sea creatures every year.

Global warming

Our planet is getting gradually hotter. This is called global warming. It is caused by carbon dioxide in the Earth's atmosphere. Many scientists believe we must cut carbon dioxide emissions to slow down global warming. These emissions mostly come from burning fuel to create energy–such as when we use oil to run cars or burn coal to create electricity or make heat.

More than 1 million species have become extinct because of global warming.

TAKE ACTION!

A simple eco-friendly thing to start doing is to walk or ride your bicycle to school if it's possible and safe for you. This cuts fuel usage, which means lower carbon dioxide emissions and less pollution. And it's healthy for you too.

Our rivers and lakes

Many of us are lucky to have clean running water in our homes. But by 2025, according to USAID (the United States Agency for International Development), one third of the world's population will face water shortages because of river and lake pollution and also because of global warming, which in turn causes climate change.

STOP AND THINK!

Planet Earth is home to about 7.5 billion people. All of us rely on this amazing planet for the air we breathe, the water we drink, and the food we eat. We also get to enjoy its wilderness and oceans. Modern humans evolved 200,000 years ago. In all that time, the Earth has sustained us. Now it is time for us to look after Earth!

Time to Go Green!

The children start making changes in their lives. The next day, they ride their bikes or walk to school rather than going by car. At school, they ask their teacher how they can do more to help the environment.

▼ Empty milk and juice containers are brought from home and reused as water containers or as planting pots for seeds.

▼ This school gets environmentally friendly stationery whenever it can. This paper is 100 percent recycled.

▼ This is a zero-waste classroom. Recycling bins have been set up for paper, plastic, and glass so nothing goes to landfills.

▲ Paper isn't wasted here. It is cut up as scrap paper or reused to make new notebooks. Everyone writes on both sides too.

Pens and pencils are used until they wear out. They may not look shiny and new, but they do the job just as well.

Ms. Monroe is happy the children have decided to go green! She explains that going green is about discovering how the planet is changing and what we can do about it. It's also about being environmentally friendly and making choices in our lives that help protect the planet. Ms. Monroe has already made changes in her classroom to look after the environment.

▲ The children love to plant seeds and watch them grow. It's healthy to bring the outdoors into the classroom, and it reminds the children how amazing nature can be.

ORGANIC

STOP AND THINK!
Some plastics used in drink containers or bottles are biodegradable, which means that they will eventually break down or decompose. However, even these plastics are harmful to the environment and can take between 450 to 1,000 years to break down completely.

Reducing Carbon Emissions

Going green means understanding more about what is happening to our Earth and why it's a problem. Global warming, climate change, and pollution are major challenges facing the world today.

Nobody knows for sure why the world is getting warmer, but most scientists believe it is because of greenhouse gases such as carbon dioxide. Carbon dioxide is released into Earth's atmosphere when we burn fossil fuels to create energy.

It's the simple everyday things that we all do that add to carbon emissions—whether that's warming our homes, cleaning our clothes, cooking our meals, or driving our cars. The good news is that by going green we can reduce our carbon emissions.

Many of the activities that produce carbon dioxide are responsible for pollution too. If we can find ways to reduce carbon dioxide emissions, we can really help the environment.

To reduce our carbon emissions we need to think about the everyday things we do and find alternatives or make changes. To do this we need to look closely at the transportation we use, the energy supply to our homes, the energy use in our homes, the food we eat, and how we already reduce, reuse, and recycle.

TAKE ACTION!

Making changes like walking or biking to school rather than going by car will reduce your carbon emissions. Even switching off lights when you don't need them, or deciding to reuse and recycle, will reduce the energy you use. And if your home is powered by solar energy (power from the sun), you can reduce your emissions even more.

Climate Change

Every small change we make to our lifestyle helps reduce our carbon emissions, which also slows down climate change. But why is climate change such a big deal?

Ms. Monroe explains that the Earth is warming up very slowly. Since 1900 it has gotten about 1.4°F warmer. Some scientists think that by the end of the 21st century it could be warmer by another 3.6°F to 9°F.

Extreme weather alert

Many experts agree that hotter temperatures will create different weather patterns. Some experts believe that extreme weather like heatwaves, droughts, flooding, and even blizzards will get worse as the planet heats up.

TAKE ACTION!

Make your own climate! Small changes at home like turning down the heat can reduce your carbon emissions. When you feel cold, put on a sweater or move around to warm up. And when it's hot, don't switch on the air conditioning or an electric fan. Instead, dress for the heat by wearing lighter, whiter clothes and seeking shade.

STOP AND THINK!

Climate change is affecting the lives of endangered animals. Polar bears in the Arctic depend on sea ice because it's where they live and hunt for food. The temperature in the Arctic is rising and the ice is melting—perhaps by about 4 percent each decade. Life for polar bears will get more difficult as the ice recedes. Scientists fear they could become extinct.

Flood warning!

Climate change is causing polar ice to melt and sea levels to rise. In the future this could cause flooding of coastal regions and the loss of low-lying land.

Why Should We Reduce?

It's important that we all reduce, reuse, and recycle. The children want to know why it's so important to reduce waste. Luckily, their teacher is already environmentally friendly and she explains the facts to them.

Money. It costs a lot of money, energy, and natural resources to make everything—whether that's food or everyday items like the clothes we wear or the devices we use.

Transportation. Transporting food and everything we need to live costs money. And because we still use mainly fossil fuels like oil for transportation, it causes pollution too.

TAKE ACTION!

Borrow books from the library or from a friend. Rent a film digitally or buy a DVD from a thrift store. Try to buy durable items that will last so you don't end up throwing things away that end up in landfills.

STOP AND THINK!

Reducing the things you buy is the first important step you can take when you go green. Get into the habit of asking yourself if you need something before you buy it. At school there are often crazes for exciting new things–loom bands and spinner fidgets are two recent examples. But these things quickly go out of fashion and usually cannot be recycled, which means they inevitably end up in landfills. Do you really want to add to the waste mountain?

Waste. When we've finished with something or thrown it away, it costs money to get rid of it. We pay for the garbage trucks that visit our streets to empty our garbage cans and for the incineration process to get rid of our waste.

Landfills. If our waste goes to a landfill site, that causes problems too. Dangerous toxins can leak into the surrounding area.

Pollution. Toxins from landfills can kill animals and plants and get into our water supply.

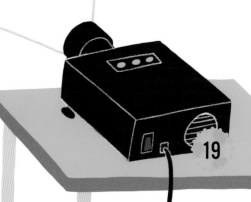

19

Why Do We Reuse?

To help the children understand why we should reuse things, the school asked Ed from a local thrift store to tell the children about his job.

Ed is an expert at giving objects a second life. People donate all kinds of things to his store—from furniture to large appliances such as fridges to toys such as teddy bears. Ed makes sure that everything is used again, rather than taken to landfill sites. Most of us throw away things that other people need or want.

One person's trash is another person's treasure!

STOP AND THINK!
Lots of used, secondhand, or pre-owned clothes that are rejected by thrift stores in the USA and Europe are sent to other nations. These clothes may not be the latest fashions, but they are in great condition and there is a flourishing market for them.

Refrigerator dilemmas

Refrigerators have a chemical inside called refrigerant, which keeps things cool. Refrigerants are greenhouse gases, which are bad for the environment. For this reason, fridges and freezers should never be thrown away or put in landfills.

Sofa solutions

Bulky waste like sofas take up a lot of space in landfills. As long as a sofa has a label with fire regulations on it, it can be reused by another family. Otherwise it must be thrown away.

Reuse fridges

Because it's so difficult to recycle or dispose of our old fridges, it makes sense to try to find new homes for the ones that are still working or can be fixed.

Hard recycling

Large appliances like dishwashers, washing machines, and ovens are difficult to recycle. They are bulky, heavy, and have to be dismantled carefully to recycle the steel, copper, and aluminum within.

Reuse in Action

The children are inspired by the idea of reusing things. At home they look for things they don't want or need anymore and find clothes, books, toys, and sports equipment that could be given away. They want to know if there is a way they can swap or exchange these things for what they *do* need.

Lulu discovers lots of websites where it is easy to swap almost anything (with an adult's help). There are also plenty of sites where you can give your stuff away or get things—for free!

The Freecycle organization began in Tucson, Arizona, in 2003. The idea was to give away unwanted reusable goods to reduce waste and to prevent so many things from going into landfills. The items were offered online and the givers decided who received an item from the responses they got. People could also post the things they wanted and let the group know when they had received the items they were looking for. Today there are about 7 million members of Freecycle groups in more than 100 countries all over the world. The rules are simple: Everything that is advertised must be free.

And sometimes you GET.

This helps the environment.

TAKE ACTION!

Encourage your family to join a local organization like Freecycle and see what you can keep from going to landfills. Everything you give away or receive reduces waste and helps reduce your carbon footprint.

23

Why Do We Recycle?

Recycling is important, too, if you want to go green. But recycling is the third R for a reason. It takes money, energy, and resources to recycle something.

To find out more, the children visit a material recovery facility (MRF) where a woman called Ava tells them how they sort the recycled products. At this center the recyclables arrive mixed together.

STOP AND THINK!
By recycling 1 ton of aluminum drink cans we can prevent 3 tons of carbon dioxide emissions.

TAKE ACTION!
Become the recycling leader of your household and learn all you can. For example, find out where you can safely dispose of old batteries. Similarly, cardboard drink cartons and certain other containers are often collected separately, and so are textiles. Discover what else is being recycled in your area–and how–and get to it!

1. The mixed recycling is tipped onto a conveyor belt. The materials are hand checked for recyclable glass, plastic bags, and textiles. These will be processed separately.

2. Now the recycled waste is separated out into different materials. The spinning action inside a big drum called a trommel will separate items like cans and plastic bottles.

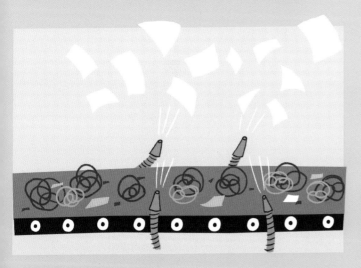

3. Compressed jets of air from a machine nicknamed the air knife separate out the paper.

4. A massive magnet draws steel cans out of the mix. Electromagnets repel the aluminum cans so they can be separated out.

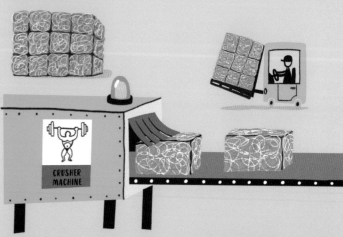

5. Infrared cameras scan the bottles to find which type of plastic they are made from. Jets of air move the various kinds of plastic to different areas.

6. A giant crusher compacts the separated materials into large bales. These bales of separated material are sold to companies that will make new products reusing these materials or use them again in industry.

The Recycle Cycle

Once the items have been sorted, the children discover what happens next in the recycling process.

BEFORE

AFTER

Cardboard → Cardboard tubes and packing

Paper → Other paper products

Glass bottles → New glass products

Aluminum cans → Signs, seating, or new cans

Batteries → Metals and plastic

Steel cans and aerosol cans → Steel sheets used in the construction, auto, and packaging industries

The children learn what their items could become once they're recycled. Old paper can easily be recycled and used again. Even tired old clothes can be used as filling for bedding. The children are amazed at the possibilities!

BEFORE

AFTER

Cooking oil → Biofuel for heating

Garden waste → Compost

Soft plastics → Backpacks, carpet, and sleeping bags

Wood → Animal bedding

Textiles → Used to stuff bedding

27

Second Chance at Life

Next the children go in search of other ways that people are recycling materials to produce ethical and eco-friendly goods. For example, the children find out that some companies are turning old sneakers into soft and safe playground surfaces.

The new and exciting life cycle of a pair of shoes . . .

Most kids love sneakers–especially if they're the latest "must-have" ones.

But every sneaker has its day when it gets too small.

You can give your old sneakers to charity or to recycling centers.

The shoes that go to recycling centers may be sent to children who need them.

Some worn-out shoes are sent to factories where the rubber soles are ground down to make a new material called *grind*.

Grind is used to make surfaces for playgrounds, running tracks, and more.

TAKE ACTION!
Look for other clothes that have been made from recycled materials. Plastic bottles can be turned into great hoodies. Inventive designers have also made dresses from candy wrappers, plastic bags, and newspapers.

29

Make It Green

The idea of upcycling—reusing parts of things to make something else—really appeals to the children. Their art teacher helps them make some cool stuff at school. Reusing and recycling things that they would normally throw away feels good and is a great hobby.

The children make an awesome bowling set from old plastic bottles. See what you have lying around, and use your imagination to come up with a unique design of your own.

STOP AND THINK!
Upcycling means reusing something in such a way that it is better than it was before. People mostly upcycle something they would have thrown away otherwise. A good example is old furniture. A coat of paint and a few new handles on a dresser will give it a different look. Upcycling like this also tends to be cheaper than buying new.

30

MAKE AN AWESOME BOWLING SET!

What you need:

x10 10 plastic bottles or other containers of the same shape and size

Paint, stickers, glitter, or anything else you can find for decoration

 Glue

 Water or sand to fill the bottles

Ball

Instructions:

1. Clean the bottles and remove all the lids. Put the lids in a safe place for later.

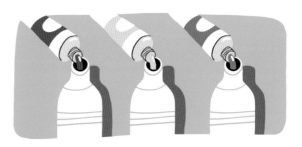

2. Squirt a different colored paint into each bottle. If the paint is thick you can add a little water to the paint.

3. Put the lids back on the bottles and get ready to shake. Shake each bottle until the paint coats the whole inside of the bottle.

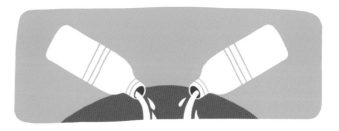

4. Remove the lids from the bottles and pour out any extra paint (ask an adult where to do this).

5. The decoration doesn't have to end there. Add ribbon or glitter to the outside. Paint faces or make interesting creatures out of each bottle. Let your bottles dry overnight.

6. Fill the bottles halfway with sand or water and put the lids back on securely. Your set is ready to go!

Eco Action Outside

One day Mario, from another local green organization, comes to school to talk about how the children can be more environmentally friendly on the school playground. He is really impressed by everything they do already—especially the vegetable patch. He shows them how to make their own compost heap so they have good quality compost to use on their crops.

▲ These wildflowers really get things buzzing—they attract bees and other insects to the school gardens. Bumblebees are in decline and they need nectar from flowers to survive. In return they pollinate flowers and vegetables.

▲ Tires can be recycled and used again on vehicles. They are also lots of fun on a playground. The children at this school helped design their tire-based playground equipment.

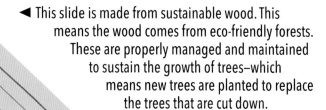

◀ This slide is made from sustainable wood. This means the wood comes from eco-friendly forests. These are properly managed and maintained to sustain the growth of trees—which means new trees are planted to replace the trees that are cut down.

Solar panels on the roof of the school generate clean energy for the classrooms. ▶

The school pond is teeming with wildlife. The children have watched these frogs grow from tadpoles. They love to come out here to inspect the pond. ▼

▲ Being green means saving water too! These water barrels collect rainwater, which is used to water the vegetables and flowers.

The children made this insect hotel from spare pieces of wood and old boxes. Butterflies and ladybugs hibernate here. ▼

TAKE ACTION!

Make compost at your school. Get together to decide whether you'll just gather yard and garden waste for your compost or collect raw and cooked food waste too. Once you've made a decision you'll need a composter fit for the job, plus a plan of action. Lots of websites offer advice on how to do this.

33

The School Lunch Challenge

The vegetables growing outside the classroom make the children think more about what they eat. And making compost at the playground makes them consider food waste.

Mr. Lee is the school cook and he knows lots of ways to be eco-friendly in the kitchen. He tells the children that home-cooked food using fresh ingredients is better for you and has less packaging than prepared food. This helps reduce waste.

Food waste is a huge problem in school cafeterias. But good, tasty food is less likely to be left uneaten. Regular changes to the menu mean nobody gets bored. And food waste bins in the kitchen ensure no food goes to landfill sites, but it becomes compost instead.

▼ Freshly baked cakes are yummy and don't have preservatives in them. Real fruit adds sweetness and flavor.

Mr. Lee shops locally for food to reduce transportation costs and energy.

Mr. Lee puts healthful food choices at the front of the counter.

MENU ♥

▲ There are lots of vegetables and salad in these school lunches.

WASTE

TAKE ACTION!

Next time you have a packed lunch or a picnic, aim for a zero-waste lunch. This means using reusable bottles and containers rather than prepackaged food and drinks in plastic, cardboard, or polystyrene. It also means reducing food waste—so make sure you gobble up everything or give it away to a friend. At school, you can compete with other classes to see who can reduce their waste the most!

The Green Team at Home

Going green at school has been fun. What about at home?

Noah is on a mission at his home. He makes sure that all the lights are switched off in empty rooms and computers are turned off overnight. The laundry is hung out to dry on a clothesline rather than being put in the dryer.

Lulu's parents installed solar panels on the roof of their house last year. These generate enough electricity to power their home. There is even a little bit left over to put back into the national grid (the network of power stations and energy generators that supply electricity in a country).

36

STOP AND THINK!
The average home in the United States has 45 light bulbs. By replacing old inefficient bulbs with energy-efficient bulbs, households can significantly reduce the electricity they use.

Traditionally, many homes have been powered by electricity made from coal, gas, and oil (fossil fuels), which create greenhouse gases and cause pollution. Solar power is a clean alternative because no fuel is burned to create the energy–it just comes from the sun.

Anjali likes to shower rather than use the bath. If she's quick, it saves energy and cuts down water use. The average bath uses about 30 gallons of water or more. A typical shower flows at about 2.5 gallons per minute.

So a 5-minute shower uses less than half as much water as a bath. Anjali never lets the tap run when she brushes her teeth either.

Mason's family uses eco-friendly cleaning products or natural products like white vinegar to clean the windows. These products are not tested on animals and they don't pollute the environment.

TAKE ACTION!

Watch out for "phantom" users! These are appliances such as computers, television sets, and microwave ovens that use power even when they are turned off. They may have digital displays or lights that draw power even when they are off. You can stop this by unplugging them.

Energy Matters!

Clean energy from the sun (solar power), water (hydropower and geothermal power), and wind is the answer to our future energy needs.

Ava from the local Friends of the Earth organization shows the children the exciting ways people all around the world are making the switch to clean energy.

Wind power

The UK is the leader in offshore wind power. Wind farms out at sea have tall wind turbines measuring about 720 feet high, which generate 7 or 8 megawatts (MW) each.

Onshore wind farms (where the wind turbines are on land) in the USA and China generate power that is the cheapest form of energy in the world.

Solar power

China leads the way in solar power production, followed by Germany.

In 2017, China opened the world's biggest solar park. The Longyangxia Dam Solar Park has about 4 million solar panels and can be seen from space! It will produce 850 MW of power—enough to supply around 200,000 homes.

Water power

Hydropower is the leading form of renewable energy in the world. It is produced by running water through turbines.

China, the USA, Brazil, Canada, India, and Russia were the largest producers of hydropower in 2015. Three Gorges Dam in China is the biggest hydropower project in the world.

Fossil fuels

The switch to clean, renewable energy is slow and it is estimated that more than 66 percent of the world's electricity is still generated from fossil fuels like coal, oil, and natural gas. These are nonrenewable sources of energy. In addition, coal-fired power stations emit carbon dioxide and pollutants like mercury, which is harmful to our health.

Water Warriors

Water is the issue Lulu cares about most. She worries about pollution of our waterways and oceans. And she is concerned about water supplies to countries all around the globe—constant, clean water is a right for everyone.

There are hundreds of organizations (most of them charities) and individuals helping keep the waterways, oceans, and water supplies of the world clean and green.

WaterAid

Every year more than 300,000 children under five are believed to die from drinking dirty water. WaterAid is an international charity working to keep water supplies clean and safe.

Teams of volunteers work together with local people in Africa, India, and other places to improve the water supply and create more sanitary conditions.

Garbage patches

There are five giant garbage patches floating in our oceans. These enormous masses contain old fishing nets, plastic containers, large plastic debris, and microplastics. The heart of the Pacific patch measures a possible 386,000 square miles. Some of this plastic breaks down and is a serious risk to marine life.

Ocean cleanup

A young Dutch inventor called Boyan Slat has founded an organization called the Ocean Cleanup to get rid of these dangerous garbage patches. He has invented a system to rid the seas of plastic.

STOP AND THINK!

Microbeads found in some toothpastes, facial scrubs, and cosmetics are a serious risk to animals and our environment. The microbeads get into our rivers, lakes, and oceans. The beads are eaten by plankton, which is eaten by fish, which in turn may be eaten by birds. Many organizations are campaigning for a worldwide ban on the use of microbeads.

Transportation and Pollution

Changing the ways we get around and the transportation we use can affect pollution in the atmosphere.

▲ Large cars, SUVs, and trucks have bigger engines and use more fuel. Diesel cars are another threat to the environment. When diesel is burned, tiny harmful particles are emitted.

▲ Old cars or vintage cars use more fuel.

There are many ways that we can drive our cars in a responsible way. ▼

♻ Carpool with others whenever you can.

♻ Plan errands carefully so that you make fewer trips.

♻ Cut out air conditioning.

♻ Join a car-sharing group or service.

Once you have a bike, cycling is free. The money you save on fuel could be used to buy equipment for your bike like panniers and luggage racks. Your family's savings can also be spent on taxis when you really need them. ▶

JOIN US AND GO GREEN...IN THE CITY!

Are buses a green option?

♻ Buses often run on diesel, which emits dangerous pollutants.

♻ However, public transportation is a good idea because one large vehicle carries more passengers and relieves congestion on the roads.

♻ Electric buses are the way forward if we want a greener option for towns and cities.

◀ Most scooters and motorbikes use less fuel than cars so they create fewer emissions.

♻ Electric cars produce fewer greenhouse gases.

♻ These cars are 100 percent eco-friendly to run because they don't add pollutants to the atmosphere.

♻ Electric cars are more expensive to buy, but they are cheaper to use.

STOP AND THINK!

Walking is good for the planet and for our bodies. Get into the habit of walking places when you can, especially with friends and family! It's great exercise and gives you a chance to see the world close up.

43

The Big Eco Festival

The children have been on a great learning journey and they're excited to hold their own Eco Festival at school. They raise funds for a local green group and for an international water charity. It's a day of clean, green activities with healthful food and recycled prizes. Who knew that zero waste and the three Rs could be so much fun?

Lemonade

WIND POWER

Calculate Your **CARBON FOOTPRINT**

Anjali has a stand selling mini windmills to promote the idea of wind power.

Noah has a "calculate your carbon footprint" stand.

Edible wall ▼

◄ Tomato

Lettuce ▲

WATERAID

Lulu is raising money for the charity WaterAid.

TAKE ACTION!

Student power! Don't wait for teachers to introduce green projects at school. If you are passionate about the environment, start or join a club or run for student council. Then set up your own recycling programs, start a vegetable plot or "edible wall" (a vertical planter filled with fresh food like lettuce and tomatoes), or mastermind fundraising events for solar panels, water charities, or other causes.

Bicycle Repairs

Mason has set up a bicycle repair stand.

STOP AND THINK!

A teacher in New York City boosted his students' attendance by getting them into growing plants in the classroom. The children's attendance in his class rose from 43 to 93 percent because they wanted to be there to care for their plants.

Glossary

Biodegradable Describes a material that can be broken down or decomposed by bacteria or other living organisms.

Car-sharing service A system in which people can rent cars for short periods of time from a pool of vehicles.

Carbon dioxide A gas which is produced by all animals when they breathe out and by plants during photosynthesis. It is also created when materials that contain carbon, such as coal, are burned.

Charity An organization that raises money for those in need.

Clean energy Energy that is created from renewable sources such as from sunlight, wind, or water. Also known as renewable energy.

Climate change The long-term changes in the Earth's weather patterns.

Decompose To decay or become rotten. Leaves and dead plant material decompose into soil.

Diesel A kind of fuel that is used in diesel vehicles.

Drought A long period of low rainfall, which leads to a shortage of water.

Eco-friendly Describes something that does not harm the environment.

Emission A discharge of something such as a gas or fumes. Greenhouse gases are described as an emission.

Endangered Describes something that is in a dangerous situation. An endangered animal is at risk of becoming extinct or dying out as a species.

Ethical Something that is moral or right. Ethical products are usually green, organic, energy efficient, or fair trade.

Extinct If a species of an animal has died out then that animal is described as extinct.

Fire regulations Rules about fire safety that must be followed.

Fossil fuel A nonrenewable natural fuel, such as coal, oil, or gas, that was created long ago from the remains of living things.

Geothermal power Electricity produced using steam from hot water wells deep underground.

Global warming The rise in temperature of Earth that is causing long-term climate change.

Greenhouse gases Gases in Earth's atmosphere that trap radiation from the sun and cause global warming.

Heatwave A long period of very hot weather.

Hydropower Electricity generated from turbines that are turned by the force of fast-moving water.

Incinerate To burn something to ash.

Incinerator A machine that burns waste material at a high temperature.

Infrared camera A camera that forms thermal images from heat rather than from visible light. This means infrared cameras can be used in the dark.

Landfill site A place where waste or garbage is disposed of in the ground.

Methane gas A natural gas that leaks from landfill sites as trash decomposes. It can be used as a fuel but it is also a greenhouse gas.

Microbeads Tiny, solid plastic particles that are regularly used in cosmetics and cleaning products. These are washed away down our sinks but end up back in lakes and oceans causing problems for marine life.

Microplastics Small plastic pieces or particles caused when household or industrial plastics begin to break down or disintegrate.

Natural resources Materials such as water, soil, coal, and wood that are found in nature.

Nectar The sweet substance secreted by flowers and collected or eaten by insects.

Pollinate To transfer pollen to a plant or flower for fertilization.

Preservatives Chemicals that are used to make food last longer.

Renewable energy Energy that is generated from sources like sunlight, wind, or water.

Solar power The conversion of energy from sunlight into electricity.

Sustainable Something that can be used in the present time and be easily replaced so that it can be used in the future too.

Toxin A poisonous substance.

Upcycling Reusing something and turning it into something better.

Zero waste To achieve zero waste you must make sure to reuse and recycle everything that you consume. The goal is that nothing that you use is sent to landfills.

Find Out More

The Freecycle Network
freecycle.org
The global network of community-based reuse and recycling projects. The idea is that people can give away unwanted items and acquire items they need for free.

Friends of the Earth
foe.org
This international organization is working on a global scale to help protect our world. You can join campaigns like Save the Bees and many others to do your bit for a greener world.

Greenpeace
greenpeace.org
This worldwide charity has been actively involved with green causes since it was started in 1971. Today, among other campaigns, it is working toward stopping climate change, defending the oceans from plastic pollution, protecting rainforests, and saving the Arctic.

NOVA
pbs.org/wgbh/nova/topic/earth
Learn more about our amazing planet from this PBS website for the TV series NOVA. It offers recent episodes and articles about topics related to planet Earth.

Reduce, Reuse, Recycle
epa.gov/recycle
This website from the Environmental Protection Agency (EPA) gives lots of information on how to recycle as well as how to reduce and reuse.

WaterAid
wateraid.org
This international organization works around the world to supply clean water, proper sanitation, and good hygiene to communities that need help.

Index